A MUCHA JOURNAL

based on the designs of
ALPHONSE MUCHA

Published by Pomegranate Communications, Inc.
Box 6099, Rohnert Park, California 94927, U.S.A.
800 227 1428; www.pomegranate.com

Journal with embossed leather cover
Catalog No. AA115
ISBN 0-7649-1684-X

Journal refill only
Catalog No. AA121
ISBN 0-7649-1701-3

Available in Canada from Canadian Manda Group
One Atlantic Avenue #105, Toronto, Ontario M6K 3E7, Canada

Available in the U.K. and mainland Europe from Pomegranate Europe Ltd.
Fullbridge House, Fullbridge, Maldon, Essex CM9 4LE, England

Available in New Zealand from Randy Horwood Ltd.
P.O. Box 32-077, Devonport, Auckland

Available in Asia (including the Middle East), Africa, and Latin America
from Pomegranate International Sales
113 Babcombe Drive, Thornhill, Ontario L3T 1M9, Canada

Front-cover embossed design:
Adapted from Alphonse Mucha's illustrations in *Documents décoratifs*, 1902

Designs within adapted from the following works of Alphonse Mucha:
Documents décoratifs, 1902
La Samaritaine, 1897
Combinaisons ornementales, 1901

Cover and interior design by Shannon Lemme

Printed in Korea

10 09 08 07 06 05 04 03 02 01   10 9 8 7 6 5 4 3 2 1

DESTINED for the priesthood by his father, Alphonse Mucha (Czech, 1860–1939) instead became one of the most renowned poster designers of the Art Nouveau period. As a boy, Mucha exhibited artistic talent. After he graduated from high school, several of his sketches caught the eye of a local aristocrat, who subsequently paid for Mucha's schooling in Paris.

Le style Mucha was launched on Christmas Eve, 1894. Mucha was checking proofs for a friend at a printing company when Sarah Bernhardt telephoned, demanding a different poster for her production of *Gismonda,* to be launched on New Year's Day. No other artists were available, so Mucha got the job and created a poster that, once displayed on billboards, immediately became a collector's piece because the design was so unique.

Mucha produced postcards, panels (his *panneaux décoratifs*), stamps, and commercial products in addition to his celebrated posters. His designs involve exotic motifs, beautiful women, and flowing lines. Always a fiercely patriotic Czech, from 1912 to 1928 Mucha devoted himself to *The Slav Epic,* which celebrates the spirit of his people; the work consists of twenty huge panels in tempera and oil.

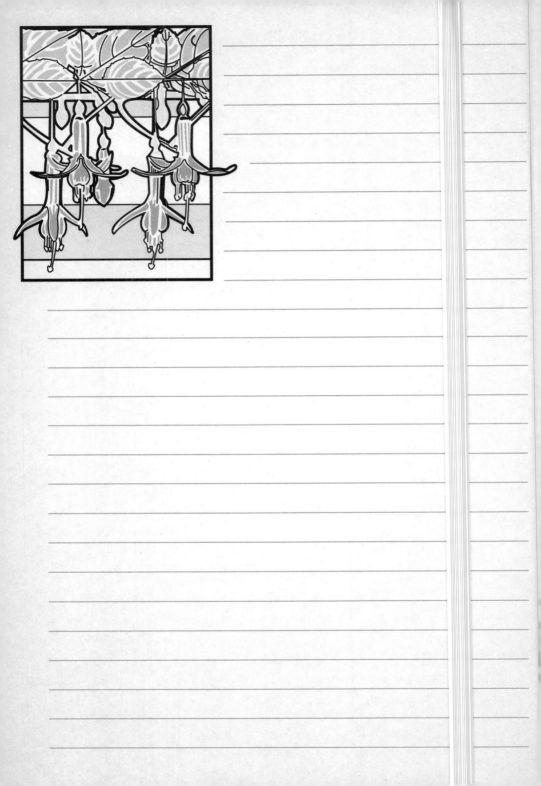

For replacement journal inserts please visit your local retailer or order direct from Pomegranate by calling 800-227-1428 or by visiting our website at www.pomegranate.com.